In the Spotlight

P!nk

by Kaitlyn Duling

Ideas for Parents and Teachers

Bullfrog Books let children practice reading informational text at the earliest reading levels. Repetition, familiar words, and photo labels support early readers.

Before Reading

- Discuss the cover photo. What does it tell them?

- Look at the picture glossary together. Read and discuss the words.

Read the Book

- "Walk" through the book and look at the photos. Let the child ask questions. Point out the photo labels.

- Read the book to the child, or have him or her read independently.

After Reading

- Prompt the child to think more. Ask: What did you know about P!nk before reading this book? What more would you like to learn about her after reading it?

Bullfrog Books are published by Jump!
5357 Penn Avenue South
Minneapolis, MN 55419
www.jumplibrary.com

Library of Congress Cataloging-in-Publication Data

Names: Duling, Kaitlyn, author.
Title: P!nk / by Kaitlyn Duling.
Description: Minneapolis : Jump!, Inc., [2019]
Series: In the spotlight
Series: Bullfrog Books | Includes index.
Identifiers: LCCN 2018018925 (print)
LCCN 2018020698 (ebook)
ISBN 9781641282031 (e-book)
ISBN 9781641282017 (hardcover : alk. paper)
ISBN 9781641282024 (pbk.)
Subjects: LCSH: P!nk, 1979—Juvenile literature.
Singers—United States—Biography
Juvenile literature.
Classification: LCC ML3930.P467 (ebook)
LCC ML3930.P467 D85 2019 (print)
DDC 782.42164092 [B]—dc23
LC record available at https://lccn.loc.gov/2018018925

Editor: Susanne Bushman
Designer: Molly Ballanger

Photo Credits: JB Lacroix/Getty, cover; Jeff Kravitz, 1, 9; Kevin Winter/Getty, 3; Tibrina Hobson/Getty, 4, 23tr; Kevin Mazur/Getty, 5, 6–7, 10–11, 14, 23bl, 23bm, 23br; DWD-Media/Alamy, 8, 23tl; Jason Merritt/Getty, 12–13, 23tm; Paul Zimmerman/Getty, 15; C Flanigan/Getty , 16–17; Jesse Grant/Getty, 18–19; Jack Fordyce/Shutterstock, 20–21; Ron Galella/Getty, 22l; ricochet64/Shutterstock, 22tr; Album/Alamy, 22b; Taylor Hill/Getty, 24.

Printed in the United States of America at Corporate Graphics in North Mankato, Minnesota.

Table of Contents

P!nk

This is Alecia Beth Moore.

We call her Pink.

She spells it P!nk.

She is famous!

She is a singer.

She writes songs.

P!nk

She performs.
She does tricks in the air.
Wow!

She sells albums.

album

She wins awards.

award

Fans love her music.

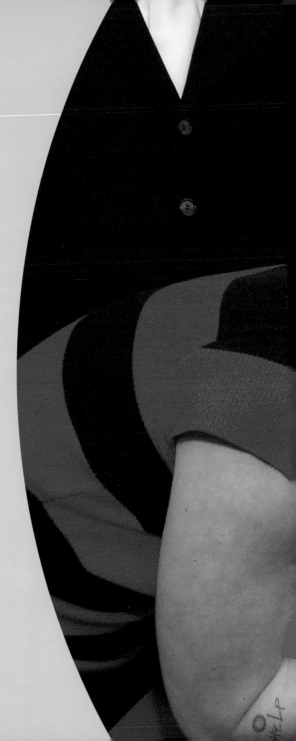

fan

THE MARGIE PETERSEN
BREAST CENTER
AT SAINT JOHN'S HEALTH CENTER

Restoring health while treating disease

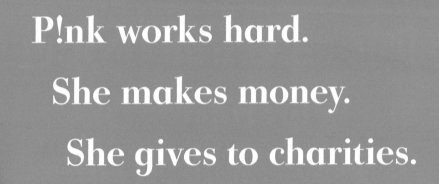

P!nk works hard.
She makes money.
She gives to charities.

P!nk works with UNICEF.

She helps raise money for kids.

14

She helps kids be active.

15

Her daughter is Willow.

She teaches Willow
to help.

Willow

P!nk loves animals, too.
She gives time and
money to help them.

Way to go, P!nk!

Key Events

September 8, 1979:
Alecia Beth Moore is born in Doylestown, Pennsylvania.

December 5, 2000:
P!nk wins Female New Artist of the Year at the Billboard Music Awards.

November 30, 2015:
P!nk is named a UNICEF ambassador.

April 4, 2000:
P!nk releases her first album, *Can't Take Me Home.*

November 18, 2011:
Happy Feet Two is released, featuring P!nk as the voice of Gloria.

September 2017:
P!nk donates $500,000 to the American Red Cross to help after Hurricane Harvey.

Picture Glossary

albums
Collections of music.

charities
Organizations that help people in need or some other worthy cause.

famous
Very well-known to many people.

fans
People interested in and enthusiastic about something or someone.

performs
Entertains a group of people.

UNICEF
A program that helps kids and mothers around the world.

Index

To Learn More

Finding more information is as easy as 1, 2, 3.

❶ Go to www.factsurfer.com

❷ Enter "P!nk" into the search box.

❸ Click the "Surf" button to see a list of websites.